A STUDY GUIDE
ON THE
TEACHINGS

by

MACK B. STOKES
Associate Dean
and
Parker Professor of Systematic Theology
Candler School of Theology

tidings

1908 Grand Ave., Nashville, Tenn. 37203

TO

THE MINISTERS AND LAYMEN

OF

THE HOLSTON CONFERENCE

PREFACE

This little book was first prepared at the request of the Quadrennial Emphasis Committee of the Holston Conference. It aims to lift up the major teachings of Jesus about God, man, the kingdom, and the way or style of life, which have a primary bearing on the people of Christ as agents of love and reconciliation. It is designed for use in local churches and in small Christian groups.

I wish to recognize my indebtedness to my friends and colleagues of the Holston Conference by dedicating this little book to them. I am indebted also to Dr. Emerson Colaw who, upon reading it, desired for it a wider use in The United Methodist Church and, to that end, submitted it to the Editor of Tidings for possible republication. I wish to express appreciation to Dr. William A. Beardslee and Dr. Arthur W. Wainwright—distinguished New Testament scholars of Emory University—for valuable suggestions. To my secretary, Mrs. Oviatt, I express appreciation for preparing the manuscript through its many revisions.

Mack B. Stokes

Candler School of Theology
Emory University, 1970

TABLE OF CONTENTS

I

Introduction

Preliminary Remarks

1. Many questions are being asked about the life and teachings of Jesus.
   a. Do we really know what he was like?
   b. Can we be sure of what he taught?
   c. Does it matter whether we know what Jesus said and did? After all, why not go ahead and have faith in God anyway?
2. Long before these questions were widely asked by men today they have been raised and studied by scholars. In fact, during the past two hundred years these and similar questions have been discussed at great length among Biblical scholars and teachers. Every seminary student has been exposed to them.

I. Three views on the historical Jesus.

1. As we might suppose, Biblical scholars have come up with a variety of answers concerning what we can know about Jesus. I shall begin with brief statements on two opposing views which scholars have held. Then I shall turn to a third scholarly view which, in my judgment, gives us the most sound approach to the life and teachings of Jesus that we can have today.
   a. *The first view* was developed primarily by scholars during the nineteenth century.

    i. They tended to agree that we know in detail what Jesus said and did.

    ii. Some of them insisted that we can present to the church and the world clear and convincing biographies of Jesus. So they wrote many books on the life of Jesus. They contributed much to the study of Jesus and his teachings.

    iii. But, their work has failed to convince.

b. *The second view*—which prevailed during the first half of the twentieth century—assumed that a true understanding of the life and teachings of Jesus was neither possible nor necessary for faith. That is, many scholars insisted that we do not know much about Jesus, but we can go on in the life of faith anyway. Because of the present influence of this skeptical perspective we need to take a closer look at it. Besides, skeptical thoughts about Jesus are no longer confined to a few isolated scholars. They pervade the thinking of millions of people, including many well educated men and women. Therefore, we must strive to understand what is involved.

    i. We might ask: Why would people—especially Biblical scholars—let themselves become so skeptical? Do we not have Matthew, Mark, Luke and John? Are they not reports on what Jesus said and did? Why all the doubt, then?

    ii. This is a long story. We cannot do more than begin to tell it. From the start it must be clear that nearly all of these doubts have been honest. Most of them have been raised by men who themselves were and are dedicated Christians.

        Such doubts about Jesus are possible because we have to depend on others for everything we know about him. As F. W. Beare says:

        In any serious study of the Gospels, we have always to keep in mind that Jesus himself left nothing in writing, and that the earliest records of his career which have come down to us were not put into writing until forty years after his death. All our knowledge of him is drawn from the deposit of tradition which was transmitted for several decades by word of mouth (*The Earliest Records of Jesus,* p. 16).

iii. Against this background we may ask, what were some of the main reasons for doubting that we can know who Jesus was or what he said and did? Let me mention four:

1) First, they said that the four gospels (Matthew, Mark, Luke and John) were not primarily intended to present facts about Jesus. They were designed to present the gospel or good news.

2) Second, the gospels were brought together out of materials which were used in Christian communities. So the gospel materials were divided by scholars into many units. These were studied with a view to seeing what purpose each unit served in the communities of faith. For example, how were the parables of the sower, the prodigal son, and others used in the churches? How were the sayings in the Sermon on the Mount employed in the worship and life of the early Christians?

Another way of saying this is to suggest that the four gospels were not written by reporters who followed Jesus around and, afterwards, recorded what he said and did. Rather, they are made up of *units* of materials which had been circulating in Christian communities. Many years after the death of Jesus these were brought together by the four evangelists called Matthew, Mark, Luke and John.

3) Third, many scholars said that often the gospel materials are legendary or mythological. So they cannot be accepted by men in the twentieth century. This was said, for example, about most of the miracles of Jesus.

Along this line, some scholars urged that the difficulty goes much deeper than the miracle stories. The real problem is that the writers of the four gospels lived in a different world from men today. So their whole perspective, we were told, was infected with mythological modes of thought.

This argument can be summarized by saying that the four gospels are like stained-glass windows which picture not what Jesus was really like but what the early Christians, with their ancient perspectives, imagined him to be. Besides all this, after the resurrection of Jesus their primary interest was to present their risen Lord rather than the historical figure, Jesus of Nazareth.

4) A fourth reason why these scholars were willing to go along with these skeptical conclusions about the historical Jesus is that they believed that men could still find room for the life of faith. In fact, they suggested that we are now more free than ever to live by faith as members of the Christian community.

All we really need to know about Jesus are three things: (i) First, he presented the good news that the kingdom of God is promised to all men in the immediate future; (ii) Second, he called men to respond in faith and obedience *now;* and (iii) Third, he communicated the urgency of this, as no one else has done, by his passion and death. (Generally speaking, those who have followed this line have denied the resurrection as an historical event. They have tended to reduce the reports of the resurrection of Jesus to interpretations of the life and death of Jesus intermingled with the hope of the early Christian community for the life to come.)

The faith of the early Christians, so we were told, was not in the man, Jesus of Nazareth. Rather, it was in the One whom they thought of as their risen Lord, the Christ of faith.

    iv. This general perspective also has resulted in the need for further study and rethinking.

c. In the light of these two ways of looking at Jesus and the gospels, *a third and,* in my judgment, *a more convincing approach* has been emerging. This is made possible by the earlier studies of Jesus even though, taken as a whole, they ended in failure.

    i. There are now new efforts among scholars to get back to the historical Jesus and his teachings.

    ii. All are agreed that a detailed biography of Jesus cannot be written.

iii. Nearly all are agreed that the only way back to the historical Jesus is through the four gospels and other New Testament writings, which were written and preserved within and for the ancient Christian communities of faith.

iv. But many of those who are engaged in the new efforts to study what Jesus said and did are convinced that we can gain *an essentially accurate account of what Jesus was like through the reports and witnesses of the early Christians.* We can bring together also a basically reliable summary of what he taught. In other words, the four gospels and other references to Jesus in the New Testament contain enough historical materials for us to construct an authentic account of Jesus and his ministry. There is another source, the Gospel of Thomas, which has been of some help.

v. This third scholarly approach, to which I subscribe, may be summarized by saying that the four gospels (especially the first three) and the many references to Jesus in other parts of the New Testament present with essential validity what Jesus was like.[1]

vi. How far these new efforts will get among scholars remains to be seen. But there are many first-rate writers on the New Testament today who are convinced that we can get an accurate understanding of Jesus by looking through the eyes of the earliest Christians.

2. There are passages in the four gospels which, on any view, cannot be interpreted with certainty. Sometimes there are indications of later interpolation and of interpretations for the benefit of the early Christians. But, with all the aids of modern

---

[1] Among the best brief scholarly presentations of this conclusion that I know are these: Joachim Jeremias, *The Problem of the Historical Jesus*, tr. Norman Perrin (Philadelphia: Fortress Press, 1967) 24 pages; Hugh Anderson, *Jesus and Christian Origins* (New York: Oxford University Press, 1964) Chapter II; Reginald H. Fuller, *The New Testament in Current Study* (New York: Charles Scribner's Sons, 1962), Ch. II; A. M. Hunter, *The Work and Words of Jesus* (Philadelphia: Westminster Press, 1950), Ch. I. For my own statement on this, see *The Epic of Revelation* (New York: McGraw-Hill, 1961), pp. 146-150.

scholarship, these gospel materials and other writings in the New Testament show that the historical Jesus was of utmost importance to the early Christians. Consequently, included in their writings is an effort to preserve an historically reliable account of Jesus and his teachings.

Since Jesus left no writings, it is self-evident that we must see him through the eyes of those who were close enough to him in time and affection to write about him.

II. At this point I want to state seven presuppositions of this guide to the teachings of Jesus; these, which will be assumed as basic, are:

1. First, I shall assume that Jesus was incomparably greater than those who wrote about him in Matthew, Mark, Luke and John. Therefore, neither they nor the Christian groups to which they belonged could have constructed the sayings, the parables, and the responses of Jesus. Inferior men, whether in community or not, are incapable of creating the greatness of utterance and distinctiveness of approach in relation to others which we find in the four gospels.

   Here I am speaking generally. There are indications of later addition, changes of words and settings, etc. in the gospels.[2] Sometimes, for example, different writers seem to report the same incident differently. Now and then the people to whom Jesus was speaking, or the setting, are different. Even the Lord's Prayer and the Sermon on the Mount are presented with significant differences by Matthew and Luke (see Matthew 6:9-13, Luke 11:2-4; Matthew 5-7, Luke 6:20-49).

   Can we explain the works of Plato without Plato? Similarly, can we explain the parables, the sayings, and the events of the gospels without Jesus? John Stuart Mill asked the question long ago which answers itself: "Who among His disciples, or among the proselytes, was capable of inventing the sayings ascribed to Jesus, or of imagining the life and character revealed in the Gospels?"

---

[2] See especially on this, Jeremias, *The Parables of Jesus*, Ch. II, which is entitled, "The Return to Jesus from the Primitive Church."

This is a major reason why the views of those who are essentially skeptical—despite all their scholarly equipment—are unsound. It has been observed that men of extraordinary learning and ability often go wrong because their basic assumptions are not carefully examined.

I assume that if the sayings of Jesus, his parables and his responses cannot be adequately explained as creations of the early Christians, they must go back to him. This is true whether the gospel materials are studied as collections of small units (*pericopae*) or as basic general sources. Jesus alone explains their appearance at all. And this is the assumption of those who wrote the four gospels.

The greatness of Jesus can be seen also in those teachings which, like seeds, developed in and through the community of faith. Many parts of John's Gospel illustrate this, but this too is a long story. It will be sufficient to say that much that he taught could not come to its fullest development until after his earthly mission was completed.

2. Second, I shall assume that the gospels contain at least three types of materials: (1) history, (2) interpretation and allegory, and (3) proclamation.

The aim of this statement is to clarify from the start that what Jesus said and did is presented in the gospels by combining fact plus interpretation plus the call to God. It is simply not true to say that the gospel writers had no interest in the historical facts about Jesus. Nor is it true to say that this was their sole interest. Their primary concern was to present what Jesus said and did in such a way that Christians would be nurtured in the faith and that non-Christians would be converted. But they did not want to do this by distorting the real Jesus. Rather, they sought to portray him essentially as he lived, died, and rose from the dead.

It will never be easy to separate these three types of materials in the gospels because they are intertwined. Nevertheless, they may all be used rightly in understanding what Jesus was really like.

3. Third, I shall assume that the resurrection of Jesus did not turn the gospel writers away from the historical Jesus but helped

them to appreciate and understand him all the more. Some scholars assume that the encounter of the earliest Christians with the risen Christ led them to lose interest in the *man* Jesus. They then go on to suggest that their writings about Jesus report their understanding of the risen Lord and obscure the real Jesus.

This has some truth in it, but I cannot accept it as the basic truth. I believe their experience of the risen Lord made them all the more eager to hold fast in their memories to the most important things Jesus really said and did. If they really believed that it was Jesus who was raised from the dead, it would have been whimsical in the extreme for them to have lost interest in what that Jesus actually said and did. It is equally whimsical for some scholars to imagine that those early Christians were so fascinated by the risen Lord that they lost interest in the historical Jesus.

Besides this, it was only after his resurrection that the followers of Jesus began to understand how important he really was. Whenever honest men are tremendously impressed with an event—as the earliest Christians were with the resurrection of Jesus—they do not take refuge in fantasy. They strive to understand the facts. And among those facts was the inherent connection between the life, teachings, and crucifixion of Jesus and their encounter with him as their risen Lord.

If the *man* Jesus had been unimportant, nothing could have made his resurrection worthy of special attention. It would have been just another spooky event. This connection between Jesus and the risen Lord was assumed throughout by the writers of the New Testament, including Paul. They did not always refer to it explicitly because they all *assumed* it. In writing a letter home a son or daughter does not say, "Dear Mother and Dad, As you know, I am your offspring and grew up in your home." All of those early Christians assumed that *Jesus* was the risen Lord.

Precisely because God had spoken through Jesus, and because he was their risen Lord, they wanted to keep alive the authentic memory of what he said and did.

4. Fourth, I shall assume that the teachings of Jesus can be identified only by considering *all* of the gospel materials in their

interrelationship. For example, even the sayings of the Sermon on the Mount need to be understood in relation to the parables and other sayings of Jesus. Along this line I shall assume that we come closest to what Jesus taught by studying his parables in relation to his own ways of responding to men and situations. Regarding the parables, for example, Jeremias says, ". . . the conclusion is inevitable that in reading the parables we are dealing with a particularly trustworthy tradition, and are brought into immediate relation with Jesus" (*The Parables of Jesus*, p. 12).

5. Fifth, I shall assume that the best way for me to present this outline of the teachings of Jesus is by stating their doctrinal content. That is, I shall attempt to outline the teachings as ideas that can be discussed with respect to what they mean and to whether or not they make sense. At the same time I shall assume that the greatness of the teachings of Jesus is nowhere more clearly evident than in his life and death which give them dramatic and concrete utterance. The word became flesh. It is interesting and encouraging to know that the basic teachings of Jesus, so effectively expressed through his parables, his sayings and his life, are very few in number. As Jeremias says, ". . . a few simple essential ideas stand out with increased importance. It becomes clear that Jesus never tired of expressing the central ideas of his message in constantly changing images" (*The Parables of Jesus*, p. 115).

6. Sixth, I shall assume that some of the most basic beliefs of Jesus were not always explicitly stated but exemplified in his life and responses to men. For example, some of his teachings become clear only when we understand why he opposed the scribes and Pharisees, or why he welcomed publicans, sinners and Samaritans.

7. Seventh, I shall assume a deep appreciation of all sincere and difficult scholarly efforts to study the New Testament and its background. There is an amazing amount of ignorance about the Bible. Out of ignorance men say all sorts of things and make all kinds of irresponsible accusations. Churches are divided because of ignorance. Whether we like it or not, many Christians—including college and university students—now

know that exclusively literal approaches to the Bible cannot stand. There is no reason why we have to be blind and unwilling to hear just because we are Christians. Christians throughout the world, who are looking toward the twenty-first century, are to unite in study, prayer and work to the end that God's living truth in Jesus Christ can thrive among men in the modern world.

III. *Questions for discussion.*

1. Is it really important for us to know at least basically what Jesus said and did?
2. What are your main reasons for saying "yes" or "no" to question No. 1?
3. What are the most reliable ways, if there are any, of coming to know what Jesus was like?
4. Should it bother us to know that we do not have direct access to Jesus but must understand him through his early followers? Why? Why not?

II

God as Father

Introduction

1. The most important teaching of Jesus about God is that he is Father; therefore, men should think of him, pray to him, and serve him as their Father. This, together with what it implies about the kingdom or reign of God, is the life-blood running through the Sermon on the Mount and the parables. (The Sermon on the Mount, of course, was not a single sermon but a collection of what Jesus had repeated on many and various occasions.)

2. The two most important developments in the long history of man's understanding of God are these:
   a. First, the development from polytheism (the belief in many gods) to monotheism (the belief in one God).
      i. While there were earlier hints of this, it was brought about largely through the work of Moses and the prophets.
      ii. Many centuries after Moses, Mohammed led the way toward monotheism in the Arab world.
   b. Second, the development from vague, impersonal and even pantheistic ideas of God to the belief in a personal God.

I. The Biblical teaching strongly supports the belief in a personal God.

1. Here too the Biblical writers from beginning to end assume that God is personal.

2. That is, he is understood as having the basic characteristics of a person.

    a. This does not mean that he was thought of as finite and limited, as we are.

    b. Nor does it mean that he was thought of as having a body, as we do.

    c. Rather, it means that our ways of talking about persons are assumed to apply to God.

    d. The terms we use or imply regarding persons are these: consciousness, individuality, knowledge, love, purposive action, and communication.

    Using these terms, then, we may say that God is a conscious being who knows us, loves us, acts and reacts purposively in relation to us, and reveals himself or communicates with us (also, he knows and acts purposively in relation to his whole universe).

    e. On each of these personal characteristics of God many Biblical references might be listed. One of the best is Psalm 139.

II. Jesus clarified and simplified the belief in a personal God by calling him Father.

1. This was one of the most significant developments in the history of religion.

2. Jesus was the only founder of a world religion to teach that God is the Father.

    a. In Sumerian prayers, long before Moses, God was addressed as the gracious Father.

    b. In the Old Testament on rare occasions God is referred to as the Father of the people of Israel.

    c. Interestingly enough, a great leader of a popular Indian sect, Ramananda (born around A.D. 1299) taught that God is a loving Father.

    d. Jesus made the Fatherhood of God the center around which all else in his teaching revolved.

        i. In contrast to the predominant tendency in the Old Testament, Jesus taught that God is the Father of each person (yet cf. 2 Samuel 7:14; Isaiah 1:2).

ii. In even greater contrast to the teaching of nearly all other world religions, Jesus emphasized the Fatherhood of God.

iii. More important still, Jesus used the Aramaic word, "*Abba*," or "Dear Father"; this showed a degree of intimacy and affection unknown even in Jewish literature (on this see Jeremias, *The Lord's Prayer*, pp. 17-19).

e. Jesus' teaching on the Fatherhood of God came with freshness and force because of his own intimate experience of God as his Father. T. W. Manson comes to the point when he says:

> The Father is the supreme reality in the life of Jesus. His experience of the Father is something so profound and so moving that it will not bear to be spoken about except to those who have shown themselves to be fitted to hear (*The Teaching of Jesus*, p. 113).

3. Jesus brought this home to his followers by teaching them to *pray to God as "Dear Father"* (Abba).

a. With one exception (Matthew 27:46 and the parallel in Mark 15:34), every time Jesus was recorded as praying he addressed God as Father; in that exception he was quoting from Psalm 22:1.

b. It is difficult to exaggerate the importance of Jesus' explicit instruction that his disciples should pray to God as "Dear Father" (Luke 11:2).

4. What Jesus meant by the Fatherhood of God.

a. The Father is the Lord of the universe.

i. He is the Lord of heaven and earth (Matthew 11:25; Luke 10:21); he makes his sun to rise on the evil and the good, and sends rain on the just and unjust (Matthew 5:45); he feeds the birds and adorns the flowers (Matthew 6:26-30).

ii. He is spirit, and he alone is to be worshiped in spirit and truth.

b. God is our Father in that he *knows* us in every detail of our lives, including our needs and inmost thoughts and desires (Matthew 6:8, 32; 10:29-30); he promises the coming kingdom or new age and knows its future (Mark 13:32).

21

    c. Jesus taught that God is our Father in that he *loves* us.

        i. He is concerned for each of his children, especially for those in greatest need (Matthew 18:10-14; see also 25:34-40).

        ii. He eagerly wants to share himself and his gifts with them (Matthew 7:7-11; Luke 11:11-13).

        iii. He responds to honest repentance and a forgiving spirit toward others with a gracious act of forgiveness (Mark 11:25).

        iv. The parable of the prodigal son illustrates perfectly the Father's love for those who have missed the way (Luke 15:11-32); note that Jeremias says that this story "might more correctly be called the *parable of the Father's love*" (for his remarkable analysis of this see *The Parables of Jesus*, pp. 128-32).

        v. The Father's love is extended toward all men, rich and poor, handicapped and healthy, young and old, male and female.

    d. Jesus taught that God is our Father in that he takes the initiative to *communicate* (reveal himself), to *redeem*, and *to act creatively* in our behalf.

        i. This aspect of the Father's activity was especially revealed in the *life* of Jesus. That is, Jesus viewed himself as the medium for communicating the message of the Father's prior initiative and boundless love.

        ii. Thus it is the nature of the Father to reveal himself, his love, his resources for helping men, and his desire to inaugurate his new age.

III. This basic teaching of Jesus has four important practical results:

1. It makes clear the kind of God to whom we are to pray.
2. It shows us that the Father works with us in and through his *family or community*.
3. It implies the call to the stewardship of all that we are and have because we belong to the Father.
4. It makes us keenly aware of the Father's concern for each and every member of the human family.

IV. Questions for discussion.

1. What do we mean when we say, "God is personal"?
2. How is the idea of God as Father related to him as personal?
3. In what ways does Jesus' understanding of God as Father become important in prayer?

III

God's Kingdom or New Age

Introduction

1. We have seen that the Father, as Jesus understood him, is not some far-off deity unconcerned about his children.
2. The Father Jesus talked about is active, dynamic, concerned, headed somewhere—never passive and indifferent.
3. The basic question, then, is: What was the Father doing that was so important? Toward what great end was he moving?

I. Some preliminary comments on the reign of God are needed.

1. Among the Jews there had long been the vision of the Messianic age—the new era of God's reign; this was a sustained hope.
2. Even the Samaritans were looking for the Messiah (John 4:25).
3. Among the Jews the new age was usually thought of as a political deliverance made possible by a new Moses or David (yet there were some who thought of the descent of a supernatural Son of Man).
4. In speaking of the Father's new age Jesus recovered this vision and gave it a meaning contrary to the general expectations of the Pharisees and other religious leaders of his day.
5. To the question: What was the Father doing that was of utmost importance? Jesus gave the answer: He was revealing and in-

augurating his new era or reign; this he spoke of as the "kingdom of God."

a. This phrase, "the kingdom of God," is central in the teaching of Jesus.

b. But it is not easy to say exactly what Jesus meant by it.

c. For example, A. M. Hunter says, "The odds are that if we ask half a dozen men what they mean by the phrase, we shall get half a dozen different answers" (*The Work and Words of Jesus*, p. 68). He then goes on to list various views on the kingdom of God and on how it is to come (pp. 68-69).

d. Nevertheless, we must strive to understand because Jesus' teaching on the kingdom of God is the key to nearly everything he said and did.

II. *What did Jesus teach about the Father's new age or realm?*

1. At the outset the best clue to Jesus' teaching on the Father's new era is found by referring back to the Book of Isaiah (see on this A. M. Hunter, *op. cit.*, pp. 70-72; see also J. Jeremias, *The Parables of Jesus*, pp. 115-116).

2. Jesus taught that the prophets' vision of the Messianic age was now beginning; God's reign was very near, present; its benefits were now manifest and available.

3. Jesus taught that it was his unique mission to be the One through whom the Father was inaugurating the new era.

a. It was Jesus himself—and consequently the early Christian communities—who made it impossible to separate the coming of the kingdom from his own life and mission.

b. That mission was to bring the good news of God's boundless and available love to all men.

4. Jesus related his mission to the views on God's new age found in the Book of Isaiah.

a. John the Baptist sent two of his own followers to ask Jesus, "Are you he who is to come, or shall we look for another?"

Jesus responded by making use of ancient prophetic visions of the Messianic age (Isaiah 29:18-19; 35:5-6; 61:1). He said: "Go and tell John what you have seen and heard: the

25

blind receive their sight, the lame walk, lepers are cleansed, and the deaf hear, the dead are raised up, the poor have good news preached to them. And blessed is he who takes no offense at me" (Luke 7:19, 22-23).

b. Very early in his public ministry Jesus went into the synagogue in his home town of Nazareth on the Sabbath day. Evidently he was asked to lead in the service. He was given the Book of Isaiah. He found the place from which he wanted to read (Isaiah 61:1-2) which expresses the Messianic vision in terms similar to those he used in response to the followers of John the Baptist. After reading this passage, he added, "Today this scripture has been fulfilled in your hearing" (Luke 4:16-21).

5. Jesus taught that when he himself was present and active the Father's reign was "at hand"; it became manifestly present to those with eyes to see (Luke 10:23-24).

a. According to Mark, Jesus began his public ministry by saying, "The time is fulfilled, and the kingdom of God is at hand; repent and believe in the gospel" (Mark 1:15).

b. Against the background of the key passages in Isaiah this would seem to mean that the final end of purpose of God— *the eschaton*—is now beginning to be realized (hence the term, first used by C. H. Dodd, "realized eschatology"). W. G. Kümmel states that God's reign was already making itself present in Jesus. He says: ". . . we are able again and again to establish the fact that Jesus saw this future eschatological consummation to be effective already in the present in that the *eschaton* showed itself effective in his own person" (*Promise and Fulfillment*, p. 105).

c. The reign of God is here as the Father's gift to his children through Jesus.

6. Jesus taught that the coming of the Father's new era was not a human achievement—like an improved society, better housing, etc., though these should result from the coming of the kingdom. Rather, *it was the Father's present gracious availability, in and through Jesus,* to all men and especially to sinners and needy people.

7. Another way of putting it is to say that the Father's infinite love

and purpose were now clarified and made concrete in the person of Jesus of Nazareth; these were now manifest, visible, for all who were open to the divine revelation.

a. The Father's reign was not to be seen in destructive displays of physical power as in diseases, hurricanes and earthquakes, or in rebellion and force, as the Zealots supposed (not by power nor by might); therefore, Jesus defeated the temptation to become a political Messiah (Matthew 4:8-10).

b. Nor was the Father's reign a realm of legalism, outward works and religious rites—with no room for sinners and other outsiders—as the Pharisees supposed.

c. Rather, it was the *gift of grace through Jesus now* to all who would respond, including the poor, the needy, the sinner and the excluded. The forgiveness of sins was the supreme gift of the Father through Jesus and a sure sign of the Messianic age. Hence, in Jesus' acts of accepting and forgiving sinners the Father's reign was present and manifest; no one was excluded in the Father's sight (Matthew 9:10-13; 11:28-30).

d. This explains why Jesus' ministry of healing and of proclaiming the good news of God's forgiving and empowering love to all becomes central (for a reasonable statement on the miracles of Jesus, see A. M. Hunter, *op. cit.*, pp. 54-59).

III. *Amplification of this theme by some references to the parables of Jesus.*

1. Jeremias points out that all of the elaborate parables of Jesus were used first to justify (against the Pharisees and others) his mission and preaching to sinners, to the poor, to the needy, to the outsiders. Of the parables containing the good news Jeremias says:

> ... their main object is not the presentation of the gospel, but defence and vindication of the gospel; they are controversial weapons against the critics and foes of the gospel who are indignant that Jesus should declare God cares about sinners, and whose special attack is directed against Jesus' practice of eating with the despised (*The Parables of Jesus,* p. 124).

2. Even the parable of the prodigal son was in part a vindication of Jesus' preaching of the good news to the poor and despised. It illustrates further how seriously Jesus took his mission to proclaim the boundless love of God. This is evident in many of the parables and sayings of Jesus.

This defense of Jesus' proclamation of the almost inconceivable goodness of the Father is evident especially in the following parables: the lost sheep (Luke 15:4-7); the good employer (Matthew 20:1-15); the Pharisee and the publican (Luke 18:9-14); the two debtors (Luke 7:41-43).

But, of course, there would have been no need for Jesus to defend his mission through these parables had he not been actually preaching and teaching the good news of God's boundless love to sinners and all men. This he did primarily by direct sayings, by similes, by figures, by invitations to follow him, by calls to repent and trust God, and by deeds of healing and mercy, etc. And, of course, some of the parables were directed to his followers to communicate the Father's limitless patience and graciousness (see, for example, Luke 11:5-8; 18:2-8). Other parables were given to warn people of the urgency of their plight. But our main interest for the moment is in Jesus' use of certain elaborate parables to defend himself as the bearer of the Father's good news.

3. This approach to these parables is very important in getting back to what Jesus was really saying; for who would spend so much effort in justifying his mission against his critics if that mission were not his one most impelling concern? At the same time we must remember that these parables disclose also the nature of the good news Jesus was proclaiming.

4. In being the embodiment and bearer of this good news to all men here and now, Jesus was necessarily cutting across the generally accepted notions as to the aims of God for men. Hence, there was the inevitable movement of events toward his death.

IV. *Did not Jesus teach also that the kingdom of God was in the future?*

1. This topic will be discussed further under the theme of the life everlasting.

2. Suffice it to say that the kingdom to come, whether on earth or in heaven, is an extension of the Father's reign which began in the ministry of Jesus.

V. Some concluding practical remarks on the new age begun in Jesus Christ.

1. The fact of God's new era of love is the real reason for thinking of public worship as a time of joy; it is the celebration of God's self-giving love made known in Jesus Christ.
2. This is the real meaning of the sacrament of the Lord's Supper —an occasion of celebration because through Jesus Christ God is with us both now and forever.
3. The coming of God's new age is also a call to move into the contemporary world with the mission of Christ on our hearts.

VI. Questions for discussion.

1. Why did Jesus connect his teaching on the kingdom with certain prophetic writings?
2. What are the main characteristics of the kingdom or the new age?
3. What part does man play in the coming of the kingdom?
4. What do some of the basic parables tell us about the kingdom?

IV

The Father's Concern for Each Individual

Introduction

1. Only on rare occasions did Jesus make explicit statements on the value or preciousness of each individual.
2. But nearly everything he said and did reflected his unfaltering sense of the incalculable worth of each human being.
3. Therefore, his teaching here will be brought together primarily from what he said on the Father's love for each person and from his words and responses to men in their most urgent needs.

I. Jesus taught that the preciousness of each person is grounded in the Father's concern.

1. There are sincere Christians who think that we should minimize the Father and emphasize man.
   a. They think that the real spirit of Jesus Christ is simply to appreciate and serve human beings here and now (this could be called Christian humanism without God).
   b. It has some truth in it; but it is more characteristic of the nontheistic moods of the modern world than of the teaching of Jesus.
      i. Modern man understands people in relation to *nature* (other animals, evolution; the vastness of the universe, space exploration; etc.).

  ii. Or, modern man understands people in relation to society (social sciences; man as a product and creator of culture; communism as an extreme case).

  iii. Again, modern man understands people in their psychological processes and reactions (psychology, psychiatry, etc.).

 2. Jesus understood people as brought into being by the Father's love and as made to be the Father's children.

  a. Therefore, his sense of the incalculable value of a human being was a direct expression of the Father's evaluation of every person.

  b. This is the reason why he fixed his ministry on *healing* and on *proclaiming* the good news of God's love *to those who were most in need,* that is, to those who seemed *excluded* from the concerns of God and men.

II. *Jesus exemplified all this in his whole ministry to the most needy.*

 1. In this concern for the needy he goes against a general and tragic tendency in nearly all human societies, whether ancient or modern.

  a. Whenever men have no vision of the Father's love, they lapse into groups, cliques, classes where some are on top and others on the bottom, and where the rest are on one level or another in between. Moreover, they tend to measure the worth of a man by the standards of their "in-group" rather than by the Father's love.

  b. This is a universal phenomenon in all ages.

  c. There have been the free and the enslaved; the higher and lower castes; the rich and the poor; the learned and the ignorant; the cultured and the vulgar; those with status and those without it; the strong and the weak; the healthy and the sick; the saints and the sinners; those who are in and those who are out; the winners and the losers.

 2. Many of the Pharisees of Jesus' day (to use a major example) represented this universal human tragedy *in its most demonic form;* why?

a. Because they embodied it in the very patterns and structures of their religious faith and practice.

b. They included themselves as members of the "in-group" in the kingdom of God and deliberately excluded numberless others (sinners, handicapped, poor, Samaritans) as the "out-group."

c. Consequently, man's universal pride and harshness toward his fellowmen who are more needy became built into the religious beliefs, rites, attitudes and deeds of the Pharisees.

d. The sinners, the poor, the crippled, and others were excluded on *religious* grounds.

III. *The seriousness with which Jesus regarded the situation is nowhere more clearly visible than in his deliberate ministry to the excluded in defiance of the religious leaders.*

1. He shocked the Pharisees and others by proclaiming that the Father's love is first to be made manifest toward the excluded.

a. Some were excluded because they were sinners, people who made no pretense at keeping the countless regulations and religious practices—people who also were notorious for their immorality.

i. He had table fellowship with publicans (tax collectors) and sinners (Luke 15:1-2; 19:7; Matthew 11:19).

ii. He said that the hated tax collectors and the despised harlots would enter the kingdom of God before the self-righteous and proud religious leaders (Matthew 21:31). This was not to approve dishonesty in tax collecting or a life of prostitution; rather it was to say that the Father loved these people and they would be far more likely to respond to that love than the proud members of the "in-group." How shocking to suppose that a publican could pray to God and go away justified rather than the Pharisee! (Luke 18:9-14; see also Luke 7:36-48)

iii. This, of course, was the greatest kind of shock to the Pharisees who "knew" that publicans and sinners could not possibly be included in God's realm.

    iv. Jesus revealed the Father's love by forgiving men and calling them to the new life in the Father's new era. (It is to be regretted that some sentimentalists suppose that Jesus was unconcerned about the transformation of sinners—for this reason they want to bring into the Christian community the vulgarities of language and crudities of life that went into man's sinful existence; on the contrary, Jesus urged sinners to be honest about their sins, to repent, to put their trust in the Father and to enter upon the new life.)

    v. Most shocking of all, perhaps, was Jesus' repeated teaching that the Father rejoices more over one sinner that repents than over ninety-nine "respectable persons who have not committed any gross sins" (Luke 15:7).

b. Some were excluded because they were sick, or crippled, or blind, or lepers.

    i. These were regarded by many as *obviously excluded by God*. Their condition was the surest sign that God was punishing them and had no desire to include them in his kingdom.

    ii. Jesus revealed the Father's love in his ministry of healing and hope to these people.

    iii. Speaking both to spiritual and physical needs (which Jesus did not separate), he said, "Those who are well have no need of a physician, but those who are sick; I have not come to call the righteous, but sinners to repentance" (Luke 5:31-32).

c. Others (as in nearly all societies) were excluded because they were poor.

    i. Jesus loved the poor and proclaimed the Father's love for them.

    ii. Jesus did not teach that God would reward people because they were poor and punish them because they were rich (see Jeremias, *The Parables of Jesus,* p. 185).

        1) He taught that the poor, whom the Father loves, belong in God's realm as much as any.

        2) He taught also that, while the rich belong there too, they are not likely to respond to the Father's chal-

lenge. They are too much blinded and hardened by their material possessions.

d. Still others, like the Samaritans, were excluded because of their religious and supposedly ethnic and racial differences.

2. Concluding remarks.

a. We may summarize all this by saying that if Jesus was to reveal the Father's love for *all* men, he had to begin by manifesting that love toward those who seem to have been forgotten by God and men. So this was exactly what he did. He chose the most dramatic and the most elemental way of demonstrating the Father's limitless love for his children.

b. The value we place on human beings is always measured, in the end, by the way we feel and act toward "one of the least" (Luke 14:12-14; Matthew 18:10). The Father's concern for the least is the surest sign we have of his concern for *all* his children. For we can never forget that in his sight every human being is incalculably precious (Matthew 10:29-31; 16:26).

IV. *Questions for discussion.*

1. What are some of the connections between God as Father and the value of each human being?

2. How did Jesus show his estimate of the worth of each individual?

3. Why do you think Jesus paid so much attention to the needy and the excluded?

4. How can we reflect this spirit of Jesus in our particular situation today?

V

God's Warning and Challenge

Introduction

1. Jesus included in his ministry both the warning of immediate danger and the urgent call to respond to God before it is too late.

2. As was the case with the bringing of the good news, so also in these two emphases—warning and challenge—he regarded himself as the One chosen by the Father to be his spokesman; therefore, what he did and said was the manifestation of the Father's concern.

3. Warning without challenge is worthless; more than that, it is wicked; why confront men with an impending danger unless you want to call them to an immediate deliverance? Jesus, as the One who revealed and reveals what concerns God about men, warned them that they were headed for catastrophe. At the same time he called them to repentance and the new life.

I. *Jesus communicated the Father's awesome concern over man's sin.*

1. There is a great contrast between modern man's easy conscience and Jesus' teaching on the judgment of God.

    a. For modern man sin is often reduced to psychological jargon, to disease, or to environmental pressures. There is a persistent strategy in the world today, developed consciously or unconsciously, to minimize the factor of personal responsibility in its deepest dimensions.

   i. "Alcoholism is a disease" (which expresses an important part of the truth and misses what is most important).

   ii. In the place of sin we now have anxiety, fear, frustration, complexes, etc.

   iii. Instead of sin we have environmental factors and conditioning circumstances (here too there are important truths to be retained).

   iv. Consequently, modern man has tried to create an atmosphere in which the idea of personal responsibility before God is reduced to a minimum. He wants to live in the illusion that he has "come of age" so he will not have to confront the Father who made him for his new realm; and it is this Father without whose love man is reduced to a nonentity.

  b. This same chronic human failure—though expressed differently—was present in people of Jesus' day. Hence, there was the necessity for warning concerning impending danger and divine judgment.

2. The number of occasions when Jesus warned people must be noted here in passing to show how important he thought this was.

  a. Jeremias comes to the point when he says, "The number of parables in this category is nothing less than awe-inspiring. Over and over again did Jesus raise his voice in warning, striving to open the eyes of a blinded people" (*The Parables of Jesus*, p. 160; for his detailed account of this whole theme, see pp. 160-180).

  b. Sometimes the warnings were in the form of short, terse sayings: salt that has lost its taste is thrown out (Matthew 5:13); the tree that bears no fruit is to be cut down and thrown into the fire (Matthew 7:19); the house built on sand is sure to fall (Matthew 7:26-27).

3. In all of Jesus' warnings there is the note of utmost urgency.

  a. The time to act is now, for soon it may be too late. The opportunities do not continue indefinitely. The door will shut (Matthew 25:10).

  b. The father has graciously done his part. Therefore, the failure of those who want to go on in their evil ways proud and unrepentant, will bring them under the divine judgment.

  c. Men stood condemned for their hypocrisy, their show of righteousness without the inner reality of it. Woe to the scribes and Pharisees who "bind heavy burdens, hard to bear, and lay them on men's shoulders; but they themselves will not move them with their finger" (Matthew 23:4).

4. The warnings are addressed to nearly all groups, the scribes, the Pharisees, the priests and temple authorities, the whole of Jerusalem and Israel, the rich and the privileged; all those who failed to turn to the Father were in imminent danger.

5. What stood in the way of man's response to the Father's call? What were the enemies that thus threatened man's whole destiny? Five things:

  a. First, holding to the "traditions of men" rather than rejoicing in the Father's good news for all.

  b. Second, pride and smugness that made men blind and deaf—unwilling either to see or hear, hard-hearted and closed-minded.

  c. Third, prestige and power—wanting the places of honor at feasts and the chief seats in the synagogues (Matthew 23:6); that is, counting heavily on outer show without inner authenticity.

  d. Fourth, riches and the absorption of interest in material wealth (Mark 10:25).

  e. Fifth, the unwillingness to follow Jesus who was the inaugurator of the Father's new age.

II. Jesus communicated the Father's call or challenge to all men to enter the new age.

1. Jesus, in his own person and work, was supremely important as the One through whom the Father's reconciling and recreating love was made known and available to all men. Hence, Jesus said: "All things have been delivered unto me of my Father" (Matthew 11:27; Luke 10:22).

2. What were men to do? Five things:

a. First, they were to become as little children before their heavenly Father. That is, they were to respond so gratefully to God for making known his love that they were to be able to approach him in all sincerity as *Abba, Father*. They were thus to be personally conscious of his boundless love. They were to be humble, sincere and direct in the Father's presence. They were to live and breathe the new atmosphere of that love.

b. Second, men were to be absolutely honest with the Father by recognizing their smugness, their selfishness and their wrongness toward others. That is, they were to confess their sins and have a forgiving and constructive attitude toward others in the sure confidence of the Father's forgiving love.

c. Third, men were to turn away from their sins and cleave only to the Father. For no man can serve two masters, no man can serve God and mammon (Matthew 6:24; Luke 16:13). The tree made good by the new relationship to the Father will necessarily bear good fruit. The man who puts his hand to the plow must not look back but ahead and demonstrate that the new age has come (Luke 9:59-62). Having found the one thing he was longing for, the man who seeks God is eager to give up everything else for the privilege and joy of participating in the kingdom. He has found the "specially valuable pearl" and sold all else for it (Matthew 13:45-46).

d. Fourth, out of gratitude to the Father for his love and care, men were to live the self-giving life of service to others. Jesus came to serve, so too must all the children of the Father.

e. Fifth, they were to follow Jesus as their Lord and teacher.

3. Every one who does these things will be like a house built on the rock (Matthew 7:24-25). He will suffer the opposition to the Father's new age. He will also experience, both here and hereafter, the joys of the new life in the Father's new community.

III. The Father's challenge was expressed supremely in the passion and death of Jesus.

1. Jesus, as the One with the unique mission of inaugurating the new age, was the expected Messiah, the Savior of the world.

2. The Father's challenge to his children, so marvelously expressed in the life of Jesus, was carried as far and as high as was historically possible in the vicarious suffering and death of Jesus.

3. By giving his life voluntarily, as the Father's "anointed one," he communicated, to those who understand, the extent to which the Father is forever willing to go in order to persuade men to enter upon the new life in the new age.

4. All of this, together with the encounters with their risen Lord, made it inevitable for the early Christians to move toward those doctrines about Jesus Christ which went into the formation of the idea of the Trinity. But that is a long story not to be told in this brief outline.

5. Suffice it to say that the teaching of Jesus—*through his life and death*—on the Father's boundless reconciling love for all men, had to come to *continuing* utterance among his followers. The great fact had to be regularly remembered and celebrated. So what Jesus commanded ("do this in remembrance of me"—1 Corinthians 11:24), they were eager to do.

6. This is the reason for remembering and celebrating his passion and death in the sacrament of the Lord's Supper. And, of course, it is the basic reason for preaching the good news. God's mighty act of love in Jesus Christ is both the beginning of the new age and the call to us for the total response of love toward God and all men.

7. This is the greatest challenge in the world.

IV. *Questions for discussion.*

1. How would you relate Jesus' understanding of man as of great value to his teaching on man as sinner?

2. Why did Jesus concentrate so heavily on man as sinner to be warned?

3. How did Jesus go beyond a merely cynical view of man as sinner?

VI

The Divine Strategy for the New Age: Love

Introduction

1. We have seen that Jesus inaugurated the Father's new age of forgiveness and love toward all men.
2. We have noted Jesus' repeated warnings over the failure to respond.
3. We have observed also what Jesus said men must do to enter the Father's kingdom and to participate in the work of the new age.
4. We must now consider what Jesus taught about the *way* men of the new age are to live on earth. This has to do with the "style" of the Christian (to use the language of a new fad). More deeply, it concerns the *aims and strategy* of the Christian (for the word "style" does not adequately suggest that Christians have a job to do, goals to attain). "Style" suggests that we are to be looked at or that we are to watch our ways of moving. "Strategy" fixes our minds on the goal the Father seeks to realize and consequently on *the ways and means* which have his approval.

I. Beyond reasonable doubt, Jesus taught that the love of God and man is the distinctive and controlling motive of his true followers.

1. This stands in contrast to certain overmastering aims of men in

all eras of history, namely, the desire for power, for money, and for a self-centered life without much regard for others.

2. It stands in contrast also to the absence of desire, as when people do not care about what happens to anyone. The withdrawal from responsible living in community—however much it is glamorized by the flower as a symbol—is as alien to what Jesus taught as is the frenzied passion for power and wealth.

3. Once more, Jesus' teaching on love as the master motive of God's new age is opposed to many of *the ways and means* in which men seek their goals when they are not under the Father's sway. For example:

a. Some men readily resort to physical force or violence as if this were a viable strategy. Some even suppose that physical violence can be recommended as a divinely approved way of gaining justice and equity.

   i. The Zealots of Jesus' day thought this.

   ii. This is not the strategy revealed to men through Jesus.

      1) Some have used Jesus' act of cleansing the temple—when he overthrew the table and chairs of the money changers—to suggest that Jesus used physical violence (Matthew 21:12-13).

      2) Probably no comments on this incident would convince everyone, and there are doubtless aspects of that event which are unknown to us. Nevertheless, one thing is sure: Jesus never intended his actions at that time and place to be used as his strategy for human relations.

   iii. Here we must follow the total teaching of his words, of his life and of his death in relation to others.

b. Others use methods that strike against their fellowmen more subtly.

   i. They shut the doors of opportunity in the faces of people.

   ii. Or, they ignore them.

   iii. Or, they take advantage of the weak, the ignorant and the poor by overcharging them, or by selling them inferior products, or by giving them poor service; this is the "dog-eat-dog" way; it is the way expressed in the formula: "Nice guys finish last."

iv. Or, men cheat their way through school and home and work.

v. Or, they use others as *means* only without regarding them as ends-in-themselves who are unutterably precious in God's sight.

vi. Or, they live like parasites by exploiting the weaknesses of men (dope, alcohol, sex, crime, etc.).

c. All these ways of living—however much condoned within varying segments of society—are repudiated by God and by those who by faith march under his orders.

II. The basic teachings of Jesus, as the inaugurator of God's new era, is that all men are to be loved and that the ways of living among men should communicate that love.

1. We must never forget that with Jesus everything about the way of life was grounded in the boundless goodness of God. (See Harvey Branscomb, *The Message of Jesus*, p. 107.)

2. Someone, identified as a lawyer, asked Jesus which was the great commandment in the law. Jesus answered: "You shall love the Lord your God with all your heart, and with all your soul, and with all your mind. This is the great and first commandment. And a second is like it, You shall love your neighbor as yourself. On these two commandments depend all the law and the prophets" (Matthew 22:36-40).

    a. Jeremias suggests that Jesus probably repeated this double command many times, for "great teachers constantly repeat themselves" (*The Parables of Jesus*, p. 202).

    b. Jesus added that the law and the prophets—the basic scriptures then available—were built on the foundation of these two commandments; therefore, the teaching on love was *historically* central.

3. But Jesus took what was central in the Hebrew heritage and gave it new dimensions of meaning. The Father's love included everyone.

    a. One could think he "loved" his neighbor as himself and hate the Samaritan, who belonged to a mixed race (". . . Jews have no dealings with Samaritans"—John 4:9).

b. One could imagine he "loved" his neighbor as himself and be unconcerned about the poor, the blind, the crippled, the sinner, and all in the "out-group."

c. This is one of the main reasons why Jesus went ahead with his ministry of healing and good news to the needy despite the fierce opposition of the Pharisees and others.

4. This centrality of love becomes especially clear in the words and deeds of Jesus pertaining to Sabbath observance.

   a. There were over 300 regulations on this in Jesus' day. Many of these held men down and interfered with the true meaning of Sabbath observance. Legalism had gone rampant.

   b. When the Pharisees accused the disciples of Sabbath breaking (they plucked some ears of grain and ate them), Jesus said: "The Sabbath was made for man, not man for the Sabbath" (Mark 2:23-27).

   c. What Jesus was doing here was to insist that all regulations and, in principle, all institutions were established for man and not man for them. It was the Father's love that was to be the motivating force behind all regulations. *For all authentic regulations are designed to have a life-subserving purpose.*

   d. In this extraordinary instance—perhaps repeated again and again in different settings—Jesus made the Father's love the basis for changing socially established customs and institutions. God's life-subserving love for all men had priority over the traditions and precepts of men (see Matthew 15:1-9).

5. The centrality of love reaches its highest utterance in the sayings and deeds of Jesus pertaining to one's enemies.

   a. He said, in effect, do not return a blow for a blow, as the Mosaic law teaches. If someone insults you by a slap on the right cheek, turn the other cheek. Do not resist evil men by doing what they do to you. That is do not *retaliate* in kind (Matthew 5:38-40).

   b. Opposing established ways, Jesus said, "Love your enemies and pray for those who persecute you, so that you may be sons of your Father who is in heaven . . ." (Matthew 5:44-45).

c. Jesus sealed this magnificent teaching with his own life when, while hanging in agony on the cross, he prayed, "Father, forgive them; for they know not what they do" (Luke 23:34).

III. Jesus taught that everyone should embody this principle in his life, as Jesus himself did.

1. Men find themselves, not by searching for their identity (to use the language of another fad that has some truth in it), but by losing themselves in service to others (Mark 8:34-35).
2. The greatest in the kingdom of God are not those who are always saving themselves for a crisis but those who *expend* themselves for the glory of God and the well-being of men (Mark 9:35-37).
3. Self-denial is a basic characteristic of those in the Father's new era. And it is always self-denial in the interest of the kingdom (Matthew 16:24-26).
4. Jesus himself set the example, for he came not to be served but to serve and "to give his life as a ransom for many" (Matthew 20:25-28). He demonstrated this by girding himself with a towel and washing the disciples' feet (John 13:3-9).
5. It was no accident that the earliest Christians got the message. Stephen heard it, for as men were stoning him to death, he prayed in a loud voice, "Lord, do not hold this sin against them" (Acts 7:60). Nor was it by chance that Paul could write 1 Corinthians 13. For the new era was at work in the new community of Jesus Christ.

IV. What was this love that Jesus taught by word and example?

1. It was no weak, sentimental, "gushy" attitude toward men.
2. Nor was it merely liking everybody (though that has real value).
3. By love Jesus seems to have had in mind the manly desire for God's best (both physically and spiritually) for everyone.
4. He meant also that men do not really experience this love, or express it to the full, without opening their lives to the love of God.
5. We may conclude by defining Christian love as the sustained desire, born in us of God through Jesus Christ, for God's best (both physically and spiritually) for every human being.

V. *What does this love require of Christians?*

1. It requires meditation on what Jesus said and did.
2. It requires constant nurture and reawakening through private prayer and public worship.
3. It requires the stewardship of talents, time, and money.
4. It requires sharing in the life of service to others in and through the community of Christ.

VI. *Questions for discussion.*

1. How would you define love?
2. How did Jesus respond to violence in both its obvious and more subtle forms?
3. What is the significance of Jesus' teaching on the Sabbath? How do laws and regulations serve men?
4. In what situations and toward what kinds of people does the love of Jesus especially show itself?

VII

The Life Everlasting

Introduction
1. Everything that we have said up to this point about the teachings of Jesus would be like a rope of sand without his teaching on the life everlasting.
   a. This is not to deny the practical value of his ethical teachings.
   b. Nor is it to minimize the inherent beauty and insights of his sayings and parables.
2. Rather, it is to speak in terms of ultimates.
   a. If death gets the last word, and if human life comes out at zero, how can we really think of God as Abba, "Dear Father"?
   b. Or, what practical use is there in thinking of each individual as a creature of incalculable value?
   c. Again, what kind of good news could Jesus bring to the poor and needy—or anyone else—if in the end the people who are supposedly so precious in God's sight are not worth continuing beyond death.
   d. Once more, why bother to hear the warning and call of the God who, at the moment of our greatest need, lets us down?
3. Questions like these help us to recover both the glory and the practicality of what Jesus taught about the life everlasting.
   a. His teaching gives a crowning glory to all else that he said and did.

b. It has immediate practicality because it means the almost absolute difference between living on some level of despair and on the higher ground of hope.

c. Whenever God's future looms brightly before us—like the rising sun—everything we do day by day takes on a new meaning. For in this regard hope for the future is the enduring basis for the sense of meaningful living.

4. We shall consider next what Jesus taught about the life everlasting.

I. Jesus taught that God was sure to continue what he began when he inaugurated the new age.

1. The seed implies the harvest (Mark 4:3-8, 26-29). The tiny mustard seed becomes a large plant (Mark 4:30-32). The leaven becomes the developed loaf (Matthew 13:33).

a. This is not merely to suggest the idea of gradual growth until the reign of God is felt everywhere.

b. Jeremias suggests, for example, that one main point of the parable of the mustard seed and other parables like it is to contrast the beginning with the end. "The significance of the beginning and the triumph of the end! But the contrast is not the whole truth. The fruit is the *result* of the seed; the end is *implicit* in the beginning" (*Parables of Jesus*, p. 152).

2. As we have seen, the kingdom of God was already present with the coming of Jesus Christ. He said, ". . . the kingdom of God is in the midst of you" (Luke 17:21).

3. The future manifestation of God's continuing reign in the new age will give further expression to the aims already revealed in Jesus Christ.

II. Jesus taught that the coming reign of God was very near.

1. For example, he said, "Truly, I say to you, there are some standing here who will not taste death before they see the kingdom of God come with power" (Mark 9:1; see also Matthew 10:23; Luke 22:18).

a. This need not mean that *everything* about God's new age in the future was to be realized soon after Jesus said that. What did he mean?

b. Some say that Jesus might have had in mind the outpouring of the Spirit at Pentecost.

c. Others suggest that he had in mind his own return in power after his death and resurrection.

d. Perhaps as sound a view as any is that of A. M. Hunter who says of Mark 9:1 (quoted above):

> "The clue to its interpretation is in Romans 1:3-4 where Paul says that by the Resurrection God 'appointed' Jesus as the Son of God 'with power.' When therefore Jesus says that the Reign of God will, at some not far distant date, come 'with power,' He is referring to His triumph in the Resurrection and what followed it" (*op. cit.*, p. 75).

2. Scholars differ on this, but whatever the view, the followers of Jesus are called upon to be unfalteringly confident that God's great future lies ahead of them. Therefore, they are to be eager to keep themselves under the control of Jesus Christ, the risen Lord of the new age.

III. *Jesus taught that God never intended for this earth and this present temporal order to be the final setting for his new age.*

1. He taught his followers to pray the greatest of all prayers:
   "Thy kingdom come,
   Thy will be done,
   On earth as it is in heaven" (Matthew 6:10). Therefore, every Christian must do his utmost to express the spirit of Jesus in the complex and difficult situations of this present life.

2. But Jesus called men to look toward the boundless opportunity for peace, joy, and creative adventure in the new community yet to come.

IV. *Jesus did not say just what that new community in heaven would be like, but he did say some things that are very helpful.*

1. Kümmel says, "Jesus does not *describe* the coming of God in the future; he speaks of the Kingdom of God as 'joy' (Matthew

25:21, 23), 'glory' (Mark 10:37), 'life' (Mark 9:43, 45, 47; 10:17), 'light' (Luke 16:8)" (*Promise and Fulfilment*, p. 153).

2. Jesus spoke against the Sadducees for their denial of the life after death (Matthew 22:23-33). For God is the God of Abraham, Isaac and Jacob. "He is not God of the dead, but of the living."

3. Perhaps the most meaningful word Jesus used regarding the continued existence of the soul beyond death is the word "life." Therefore, the New Testament speaks of "eternal life" or the "life everlasting."

   a. Life is dynamic.

   b. It suggests growth.

   c. It holds in it all the possibilities provided by God for an enduring and creative adventure with God.

4. Jesus taught that, both here and hereafter, God is interested in *individuals in community.*

   a. There are no isolated individuals. We are all bound to each other.

   b. The person who wants to go to heaven by himself is unfit for it. Christians seek to draw all men to God through Jesus Christ both for the blessings of this life and the joys of the life to come.

   c. Therefore, one of the most unselfish teachings of the Christian religion is this belief in the life everlasting.

V. The resurrection of Jesus was, to those who encountered the risen Lord, the sure sign of two things:

1. The Father's guarantee of the final triumph of righteousness by showing that Jesus and his love cannot be defeated.

2. The Father's administrative policy to conquer death.

VI. What, then, are the conditions for entering into the life everlasting? Four things:

1. Humility and honesty before God and men.

2. Absolute trust in the Father and in his plan for the future as revealed in the risen Lord.

3. A life of sustained love and good deeds toward all men, including especially the forgotten people, the most needy whom Jesus referred to as "the least." For Jesus' great account of the last judgment, see Matthew 25:31-46. There Jesus gave further utterance to his teaching that the new age of God was present whenever, through him, the most needy people were served. Therefore, he taught that the basis for entering into eternal life was in one's attitude toward those in greatest need.

   a. Jesus said that the sheep would be separated from the goats (that is, God himself recognizes the difference between good and bad men, and he acts accordingly).

   b. To the sheep, who are on the right hand, the King says, "Come, O blessed of my Father, inherit the kingdom prepared for you from the foundation of the world; for I was hungry and you gave me food, I was thirsty and you gave me drink, I was a stranger and you welcomed me, I was naked and you clothed me, I was sick and you visited me, I was in prison and you came to me" (Matthew 25:34-36).

      When they heard this, they asked when they had done these things. Then the King said, "Truly, I say to you, as you did it to one of the least of these my brethren, you did it to me" (Matthew 25:40).

      Then Jesus spoke of the tragic end of those who ignore "one of the least of these." (The essential authenticity of this passage—Matthew 25:31-46—is nowhere more evident than in this strong emphasis on concern for the least. What Pharisees or other religious leaders of that day would have thought of that? What Christian communities would have thought of it, if Jesus had not first taught it?)

4. A fourth condition of entering into the life everlasting is openness and responsiveness to Jesus Christ as Lord.

   a. Men may respond to the Lordship of Jesus Christ in various ways. Basically it is a matter of personal commitment to him, to his way of living, and to his community.

   b. If men have had no real chance to know who Jesus was, then the love of God in Jesus Christ is so great as to draw *all who honestly follow the light they have* into his new community.

50

For such persons are longing for God's light and, in principle, seeking the Christ.

c. Nevertheless, there is and always will be a profound meaning in Jesus' teaching that the way we respond to the Father's love—with his concern for people—makes all the difference between heaven and hell. This is his warning and his call to the new life in Jesus Christ.

VII. Questions for discussion.

1. Why did Jesus believe and teach that the life everlasting is important?
2. How did Jesus think the present life on earth is related to the life everlasting?
3. What do we know about heaven?
4. Is the resurrection of Jesus important? Why?
5. Discuss the conditions for entering into the life everlasting.

VIII

The Teachings of Jesus and the World Today

Introduction

1. Does Jesus still speak to men today?
2. I am more convinced than ever that he does. Why?
   For at least four reasons.
   a. First, his teachings are ageless.
      i. Jesus' teaching on God as Father is as necessary for giving enduring meaning and dignity to life as it ever was. And, when rightly understood, it continues to appeal to thoughtful people as a reasonable way of thinking about God.
      ii. Christian love is more urgently needed in the twentieth century than it was in the first. As we look toward the twenty-first century, we can already foresee that this kind of love will continue to be necessary in all human relations. Love is absolute. There is no way of going beyond Jesus' teaching on it.
      iii. Therefore, the call to show God's love by helping those in greatest need is one of the most urgent calls we can hear in this day of world-poverty, overpopulation, famine, and war.
      iv. Some things are neither new nor old but ageless because they are grounded in the eternal goodness of God. Such are the basic teachings of Jesus.

b. Second, the teachings of Jesus speak to men today because the basic moral and spiritual needs of men do not change.

   i. There are many new discoveries and new things. We rejoice in all of the scientific and technological advances. These pose new problems. But the basic principles of living together under God are the same as ever.

   ii. Also, the main problems of human nature and of human failure are still with us. War, crime, delinquency (whether juvenile, adult, or senile), broken homes, drunkenness, drug addiction, poverty, racial prejudice, elemental stupidity, and mediocrity—these are still with us. What is more, they show no signs of disappearing from the human scene.

   iii. In other words, as much as ever, human nature needs to be changed by the new life of God's love made available in Jesus Christ.

c. Third, *God* has revealed himself in Jesus Christ. What God has so graciously done, he will continue to make available to men to meet their ageless needs pertaining to life and death and destiny. That is, the God whom Jesus revealed will always be true to himself.

d. Fourth, the teachings of Jesus include what they *imply* as well as what they explicitly state. The developing implications of the Fatherhood of God, the brotherhood of man, the meaning of love, the resources of God's grace—these have far-reaching implications for the world today.

3. What are the areas of most urgent need to which Jesus Christ speaks today? To this question we now turn without any effort to do more than state the problem areas.

I. The first major need to which the teachings of Jesus speak today is the universal need for transformed individuals.

1. A community of selfish or bad or mediocre people will not become bearers of God's good news. Nor will they live responsibly in community.

2. The call of Jesus Christ to commitment to him and to the commission from him has to be heard by individuals today. For

they are the primal dynamic centers of history. It is difficult to exaggerate the influence on society of a person wholly dedicated to Jesus Christ.

3. This presupposes that men today, as much as ever, are selfish, mediocre, and sinful. They are wrongly related to God and to their fellowmen.

   a. They need to be forgiven.

   b. They need a new life purpose, new standards and values, and a new vision of service. These come from commitment to Jesus Christ as Lord and teacher.

4. All this presupposes also that by faith in Christ the human spirit can be changed.

   Each individual can become "a new creation," with new goals, new standards of good and bad (right and wrong), new involvements in responsible living, and a new sense of destiny (see John 3:1-7; 2 Corinthians 5:17).

5. This presupposes also that only individuals can be redeemed or brought into the life-giving faith relationship with God. This experience is an end-in-itself as well as a commission to serve. Hence, man's need for real happiness is met as he finds himself in a growing relationship with God through Jesus Christ. This is the report of millions who have verified this truth in experience.

II. The second major area of need to which the teachings of Jesus speak today has to do with men in society; that is, with community, national and world problems.

1. We have seen that only individuals can be forgiven and redeemed and empowered by grace for creative living for God and man.

   a. But the transformed individual must do his duty in relation to others.

   b. More than that, he must and will *go beyond* the call of duty to carry out the call of Jesus Christ.

2. This means that in the teachings of Jesus we are necessarily called upon to become involved with those individuals in society who are in special need. These are the poor, the ignorant, the retarded, the discouraged, the sick, the hungry, the war-ravaged

and others. They include also the rich, the prejudiced, the smug and complacent, and all who are "up and out."

3. For this reason Christians are necessarily concerned about at least nine community and world problems:

a. First, war and peace, especially as seen in any war now going on (as in Vietnam).

b. Second, racial relations and the problems involved in prejudice against fellow human beings. This is far more than a matter of attitude: it is a matter of beliefs and attitudes which shut the doors of educational, economic, cultural and religious opportunity to millions of children and adults at home and abroad.

In 1955 I stated what I would like to repeat with even greater urgency in 1970: "If God is in Christ, racial prejudice does not belong in human societies and must be cast out by the mighty power of the *love* and *wisdom* of Christ" (*Major Methodist Beliefs*, p. 83).

c. Third, poverty, overpopulation and famine. These are not confined to any race or nation. They are most urgent in the great cities and in the underprivileged nations of the world.

d. Fourth, the pollution of the air, water, and earth God has given us as our environment.

e. Fifth, the revolution in science, technology and in increased knowledge. Christians are concerned always to show the life-subserving function of all advances in civilization, including especially those in science and technology which affect communication, entertainment, space exploration and the way men live on earth.

f. Sixth, the revolution in sex. The teachings of Jesus offer the foundation for the noblest philosophy of sex the world has seen. (His guidelines can be drawn from the following references: Matthew 19:3-9; Mark 10:2-9; Matthew 5:27-32; 22:36-40; John 4:16-18; 8:1-11.) When people follow these teachings, their lives are greatly blessed; but when they ignore them, life gets cheapened. Therefore, these teachings—together with the new life in Christ—must be brought to bear upon the contemporary issues regarding sex. On the one hand, Christians are concerned about the destructive and personality-impairing expressions of sex (as in pornography and in sexual promiscuity). On the other hand, Christians are concerned to foster and promote good marriages and a sound family life throughout the nation and world.

g. Seventh, the problems of alcohol, drug addiction, cigarette smoking, overeating and the withdrawal from responsible living in community.

h. Eighth, the problems of despair, anxiety, meaninglessness and personal and social maladjustment.

i. Ninth, the problems of political irresponsibility and economic mismanagement (at home, in business, in work, in public office).

III. *The preparation of Christians for their mission in the world.*

1. Christians understand their involvement in these social issues as growing out of their prior love of God and commitment to Jesus Christ their crucified Lord.

2. They precede and carry on their work in the world *with prayer* because they know how much they and others need God's help.

3. They receive strength, renewal, and joy for their service through the *habits* of Christian living which include: public worship, study of the Bible as God's living Word, sharing, fellowship, and study with other Christians in small groups, sacrificial giving of money to the cause of Christ, and family and private devotions. In other words, Christians recognize the necessity for *the stewardship of life and possessions within the community of faith.*

4. Christians want the best information and the best know-how available in seeking to render service to their fellowmen. Otherwise, they are like the blind leading the blind.

5. Christians serve because they are so *grateful* for what God has done for them that they *have* to do their best for others. In this way they glorify their heavenly Father.

6. Christians do their work in the hope of ever greater opportunities for creative advance with God in the new era of God's reign after death. They serve under their risen Lord.

IV. Questions for discussion.

1. Are there truths that are neither new nor old? Why do you think so?
2. Why is it important for individuals to be transformed?
3. Do Christians have to be involved in social problems and community action? Why shouldn't they leave these to God?
4. How important is prayer in preparing us for responsible leadership in community problems? What difference does it make?

Selected Books

Anderson, Hugh. *Jesus and Christian Origins.* New York: Oxford University Press, 1964.

*Barclay, William. *The Gospel of Luke.* Philadelphia: Westminster, 1956.

*Barclay, William. *The Gospel of Matthew,* two volumes. Philadelphia: Westminster, 1958.

Beare, F. W. *The Earliest Records of Jesus,* New York: Abingdon, 1962.

Bornkamm, G. *Jesus of Nazareth.* New York: Harper & Row, 1960.

*Branscomb, B. H. Revised by Ernest W. Saunders. *The Message of Jesus.* New York: Abingdon, 1954.

*Branscomb, B. H. *The Teachings of Jesus.* New York: Abingdon, 1959. (Paperback)

Fuller, Reginald H. *The New Testament in Current Study.* New York: Scribner's, 1962.

*Hunter, A. M. *The Work and Words of Jesus.* Philadelphia: Westminster, 1950. (Paperback)

*Jeremias, J. *The Lord's Prayer.* Philadelphia: Fortress, 1969. (Paperback)

*Jeremias, J. *The Parables of Jesus.* New York: Scribner's, 1963. (Paperback)

*Jeremias, J. *The Problem of the Historical Jesus.* Philadelphia: Fortress, 1967. (Paperback)

*Jeremias, J. *The Sermon on the Mount.* Philadelphia: Fortress, 1963. (Paperback)

Kümmel, W. G. *Promise and Fulfillment.* London: SCM, 1961. (Paperback)

Manson, T. W. *The Teaching of Jesus.* Cambridge: University Press, 1959.

Perrin, N. *Rediscovering the Teaching of Jesus.* New York: Harper & Row, 1967.

*Wainwright, Arthur W. *A Guide to the New Testament.* London: Epworth Press, 1965.

The Interpreters Bible. Vols. 7 and 8. New York: Abingdon, 1951.

---

* Particularly suitable for laymen.

NOTES

NOTES

NOTES

NOTES

NOTES

NOTES